MASCAGNI

Book Design: Pierluigi Fasolin
Translation by: Harvey Sachs

Copyright© 1989 Treves Publishing Company, a Division
of Elite Publishing Corporation.
11-03 46th Avenue Long Island City,
N.Y. 11101

Library of Congress Catalog Card Number: 89.40443
ISBN 0-918367-30-1

''Portraits of Greatness''©: Trade Mark Reg. No. 1,368,932

Cover: Antonio Piatti: «Mascagni», oil on canvas,
Milano, Museo Teatrale alla Scala.

Facing page: Francesco Messina: bronze of Pietro Mascagni.
Ridotto dei Palchi, Teatro alla Scala di Milano.

End papers front sketckes by Ferruccio Villagrossi for
«Cavalleria rusticana», Arena di Verona season 1989.

Back papers: a scene of «Le Maschere» by Mascagni,
«Ravenna Festival» 1988.

Portraits of Greatness©
Published series of pictorial biographies
Series I: Verdi
               Mozart
               Beethoven
               Chopin
               Dante
(First published in Italian under the title ''i Grandi di tutti i tem-
pi''. Arnoldo Mondadori Editore, S.p.A., Milano, Copyright
1965.)

Series II: Puccini
               Rossini
               Respighi
               Giordano
               Gershwin
               Toscanini
               Mascagni
               Bellini
(By Treves Publishing Company, a division of Elite Publishing
Company. Each volume and title series copyrighted.)

Graphic Coordinator: Sabino Lenoci, Milano
Photografy: Giorgio Banti, Milano

Composition text: Studio SL - Via Carlo Botta, 4 - Milano.
Printed in Italy, July 1989 - Grafiche Lithos, Carugate (Milano).

PORTRAITS OF GREATNESS

MASCAGNI

by Mario Pasi
with
MASCAGNI in North America
by John W. Freeman

TREVES
PUBLISHING
COMPANY

Above, model for the world premiere of «Cavalleria Rusticana» at the Teatro Costanzi, below, the Teatro Costanzi (now Teatro dell'Opera) on the evening of the premiere of «Cavalleria».

THE BIRTH OF AN ARTIST

On 17 May 1890, Pietro Mascagni's «Cavalleria Rusticana» had its triumphal world premiere. The audience at Rome's Teatro Costanzi (now called Teatro dell'Opera) responded to it in the most extraordinary way: there were sixty curtain-calls: a real record. During the following months, the surprised world joyfully welcomed this short Mediterranean opera, the first successful work of an unknown young Tuscan. Mascagni was born in Leghorn on 7 December 1863, and he achieved fame before his thirtieth birthday - by chance, to some extent, but also thanks to his inherent worth.

By 1890 the great age of melodramma was drawing to a close with Verdi's valedictory works. At La Scala in 1887, the grand old man had returned to the stage, following a long silence, with «Otello», his second-last masterpiece. Also at La Scala, Puccini - the other up-and-coming young composer - had presented his not very fortunate «Edgar» in 1889. Catalani had made his voice heard with «Loreley» in Turin. There were various new works in France, too, but the overall mood was one of anticipation. It was an empty moment in regard to creativity, yet one rich in expectations. Audiences throughout the world were hungry for novelty and were still bewitched by an art-form that had expanded until it had reached a dominant position, and by the marvels of operatic singing.

Eighteen-ninety, the year of «Cavalleria Rusticana», also witnessed the birth of two masterpieces in the distant land of Russia: on 4 November, at St. Petersburg's Maryinsky Theater, Alexander Borodin's «Prince Igor» was finally given its posthumous premiere, and on December 19th, at the same theater, Tchaikovsky's «The Queen of Spades» - another work destined for immortality - first saw the light of day. By a singular coincidence, Mascagni as well as the Russians drew their inspiration from texts of noteworthy literary or historic importance. Tchaikovsky, the fragile and neurotic romantic re-read Pushkin, whereas Mascagni turned to Giovanni Verga, the writer who most represented the South, realism, and natural passions.

Left, the most important late-nineteenth-century Italian opera composers: Giuseppe Verdi, Giacomo Puccini, Arrigo Boito, Pietro Mascagni, Ruggero Leoncavallo, and Umberto Giordano.
Above, Mascagni at the time of the Sonzogno Competition.

MASCAGNI: A STRIKING CAREER

Mascagni's biography really begins on that evening in May 1890, which was both his birthdate as an artist and the occasion of a minor earthquake in the musical world. It must also be admitted that it was a unique, fortunate, and exemplary case, inasmuch as «Cavalleria Rusticana» was the result of a national competition; it had been chosen by a serious, rigorous commitee that included Sgambati, D'Arcais, Galli, Platania, and Marchetti.

The competition had been announced by the publisher Sonzogno in the magazine «Teatro Illustrato» in July 1888; its specific goal was the encouragement of young Italian composers. There was a wise requirement that the works submitted be one-act operas. The winners of the first three prizes were to have their works produced at the Costanzi. Mascagni won; the second prize went to Niccolò Spinelli's «Labilia» and the third prize to Vincenzo Perroni's «Rudello».

The titles alone suffice to demonstrate how much more advanced, interesting, and true Mascagni's entry was compared to the others. He had been working on another opera, «Guglielmo Ratcliff», in Cerignano in Apulia - were he had ended up for reasons we shall soon discover - and he was probably highly dissatisfied with his lot, when Giovanni Targioni-Tozzetti suggested that he set Verga's short story «Cavalleria Rusticana» to music. Mascagni said he had already considered the idea in 1884, after having seen the drama interpreted by the great, sublime Eleonora Duse at Milan's Teatro Manzoni. He worked very quickly, and the rehearsals aroused his enthusiasm: Leopoldo Mugnone was on the podium, and the singers included Bellincioni, Guli, Stagno, Salassa, and Casali. These artists would soon be able to claim, rightfully, that they had played a vital part in a glorious event. «Sixty curtain-calls!» wrote Mascagni, with hardly any exaggeration; and he told his wife, «I thought I was dreaming».

We can imagine the joy of this young artist, who had put his whole heart into his work, at finding himself so enthusiastically received by the public, the authorities, and even the queen. The other two composers disappeared: they had been swept away by the success of their incredulous colleague. He experienced a thousand joys, but he was also to suffer the torments of

a legal action that Giovanni Verga brought against him for financial reasons.

Pietro Antonio Stefano Mascagni, second of five children, was born on 7 December 1863, St. Ambrose's day. (It later became the traditional opening date of La Scala's opera season, but at that time Milan's main theater opened on 26 December, St. Stephen's day. «Cavalleria» made its debut at La Scala on 3 January 1891; it was repeated twenty-two times and was paired with a ballet, «Il Tempo», by Pogna e Bonicioli, of which nothing is known).

Mascagni's family came from San Miniato in Tuscany. It was of humble origins but not poor. His father, Domenico, owned a bakery in the same building as his home, at the corner of Piazza delle Erbe and Via Sant'Omobono in Leghorn (Livorno). Pietro's mother, Emilia Reboa, was a native of Leghorn; she died, still young, when Pietro was ten.

It seems that Pietro's father was highly displeased by his son's musical inclinations, although he allowed him

Above: the composer's birthplace in the Piazza delle Erbe (now Piazza Cavallotti) in Leghorn (Livorno); below: the composer's parents. Domenico (left) and Emilia Reboa Mascagni (right).

to attend music lessons in addition to his regular school classes. The old Latin saw, «Carmina non dant panem», must have disturbed the baker, who did indeed live by bread. But the boy's extremely lively talent couldn't be restrained. With the help and protection of his teacher, Alfredo Soffredini, Mascagni rushed through his musical studies, composed his first vocal and instrumental works, and received encouraging notices from the critics after the performance (1881) of this cantata «In Filanda», which he would recast forty years later as «Pinotta», an ephemeral work.

Before he had turned eighteen, he had become a local idol. Although his father refused to realize that his son was destined to be famous, an uncle, Stefano, provided for the young man at least until the former's death in 1881. A year later the boy left for Milan, with the intention of escaping from the provinces and entering the Conservatory.

Two more private photos of Mascagni: above, with friends from Leghorn (left), with two of his five siblings.

9

THE CHALLENGE: SIXTY CURTAIN-CALLS

Milan was then, as it is still, the Mecca of all talented young Italians, and Mascagni went from Leghorn's temperate, coastal climate to Milan's famous fog («How cold it is» he wrote home).

Milan was also the musical capital and the main center of music publishing in Italy (it still is, proportionally); it had a prestigious conservatory; the most important composers - from Verdi, the grand old man, to the young Puccini - had adopted the city; Ricordi, Sonzogno, and Lucca fought for first place among music publishers, and the centrally-located Galleria was the main meeting place for singers, impresarios, and instrumentalists of every kind.

Mascagni frequented Amilcare Ponchielli and received his advice and esteem. In those days, however, there were many good musicians, and it was necessary to make one's way, through tenacity and courage in addition to study and imagination.

Excitable Tuscan that he was, Mascagni restlessly pawed the ground. He began to understand that Milan

On these pages: above, left, a photo of the composer in his youth, below, right, Mascagni and his publisher, Sonzogno; left, an autographed photo; on this page, above, the entire Mascagni family (the composer's wife, Lina, is on the extreme right).

was a very different place from Leghorn, that everything here was bigger and more complicated, and that work and competition were no joke. Thus he decided to enroll at the conservatory - an important step in his career. He underwent the entrance examination and took on the sternest professors; but meanwhile, he gazed out the window. He became friendly with Giacomo Puccini, and was lucky enough to find a merchant from Leghorn, Count de Larderel, to help him pay for his basic necessities. Ponchielli, too, liked him very much and noted signs of talent in him.

Meanwhile, the provincial youth measured himself daily against a reality he had never even imagined. Milan's concerts left the little maestro from Leghorn breathless, and operas were performed by all the great voices of the day. Mascagni felt exalted, he listened and wrote, and he came into contact with a new world that stimulated him and made him feel that his conservatory studies were excessively restrictive.

It was in Milan that he fell in love with romantic poetry and drama. He read Heinrich Heine's «William Ratcliff» and decided to set it to music. He dreamt, he fretted, he quivered, and he did not stick to the rules; for that matter, it is true that the citizens of Leghorn are all anarchists, or nearly so, and that they cannot tolerate rules and restrictions - not even normal scholastic ones. Thus, his relationship with the conservatory was short-lived, and the divorce was a noisy one. It seems that the bone of contention was the refusal of the conservatory's director, Bazzini, to authorize the perfor-

mace of the «Dream» from «Ratcliff» at La Scala. But this was merely the straw that broke the camel's back: despite his father's anger and Ponchielli's regret, Mascagni decided that he would rather earn a living by playing in an orchestra or conducting operettas than stay in school and be misunderstood.

Was he really misunderstood by the academics? Puccini, his friend and rival, graduated, and in 1884 his «Le Villi» was performed at Milan's Teatro Dal Verme, with Mascagni playing in the orchestra. Puccini treaded cautiously, according to contemporary opinion, whereas the young man from Leghorn slipped and slid all over the place. In 1905 Mascagni was a free man, but his artistic position was merely that of assistant conductor of one Signor Forlì's operetta company in Cremona.

This was certainly not an important or formative experience, yet there was something vitally useful in wandering around the lesser-known parts of Italy, where a whole world was waiting to be discovered - a world that was sometimes grim, sometimes impassioned, sometimes charged with tension and furor. In Naples Mascagni was once forced by a potentially violent crowd to allow an encore that he hadn't wanted to allow. The company's economic situation was very often miserable: although in 1886 the junior maestro received seven lire a day - not an excessively low pay-rate in those days - he was later forced to sell the few gold and silver items he owned in order to eat (and not to eat much or well, at that).

11

TOWARDS THE SOUTH

Mascagni went southwards. The Maresca Company went as far as Cerignola in the Capitanata (Apulia), and there another rebellion took place. Mascagni could no longer stand the company, the operettas, the wretched way of life, the dusty trips. He had a woman on his mind, too - Lina Carbognani of Parma - and a baby on the way. After a furious argument with Maresca, Pietro and Lina fled, taking refuge with an Albanian community. Besides being courageous, this was all romantic and amusing. A new life was about to begin for the Mascagni couple.

«The vagabond has stopped wandering», said Pietro Mascagni's friends. «He has found a nest». The nest was out of the way but rather promising, at least initially. At Cerignola, in an area that had a healthy tradition of operatic and (above all) band music, the musician found a port in a storm, although not a permanent harbor. He taught, composed, and led the local Philhamonic Society through its first paces. Contrary to what has long been believed, Mascagni did not conduct the town band; the young maestro, whose ambitions suited the situation, tried to start an opera season. The Cerignola period had both happy and sorrowful moments for him; among the latter was the death at the age of four months of his first-born son, Domenico. But what could a talented composer expect in an agricultural enclave where people lived in the age-old way, where many were terribly afraid of anything new, and where everything an outsider did seemed eccentric? A man who comes from far away, who speaks differently, who buys himself a little dog, and who shakes up lazy local souls ends up by unleashing opposition and malevolent criticism. Yet Mascagni did pioneer work under not always optimum conditions. He did get good conducting experience out of it, but he also found it annoying. In order to get the Cerignola position he had to have his teachers in Milan send references. Bazzini and Ponchielli's wife testified to the young man's talent, and he was given a salary of 100 lire a month, which was more than decent for that time and place.

One can infer from these indications regarding Mascagni's youth that he was certainly not a stay-at-home. Unsteady and restless, he was always tempted to flee, to leave the field of battle, to seek adventure. Had he not won the Sonzogno competition with his «Cavalleria Rusticana», he would have fled Cerignola anyway. His victory merely smoothed the way for his conquest of the North, of Milan.

Left, notice of the Sonzogno Music Publishers' competition, which Mascagni won with «Cavalleria Rusticana»; below, the Maestro playing billiards with a friend.

A CHALLENGE: SIXTY CURTAIN CALLS

Tormented as he was by dull provincial life, and still intent on writing «Ratcliff» - which had become an obsession - Mascagni seemed uncertain about participating in the competition. It was Puccini who persuaded him. Mascagni worked, endured trials and tribulations, and in the end sent the manuscript off (or rather, his wife sent it for him). In 1889 he had become a father for the second time, and he absolutely needed to succeed. He was summoned to Rome to appear before the panel of judges, and he brought with him the Prelude and Siciliana, which he had not dared to send, and which he now sang and played for the committee. Awaiting the verdict was, of course, traumatic, and the announcement that he had won uplifted his heart.

The sun began to shine again and Mascagni's life became brighter. He went to Milan and looked up Puccini, who introduced him to Ricordi. Puccini had made it to La Scala thanks to his «Edgar», and he was now the benjamin of the famous publisher, who was looking for a young genius to follow the path marked out by Giuseppe Verdi. Back in Cerignola, Mascagni conducted the Prelude and Intermezzo from «Cavalleria», his admirers applauded and his enemies were furious. The newspaper «Risveglio» carried a scathing review: the two excerpts were considered insipid and boring, and there was a prediction that the Romans would be «bored to tears» when they heard the entire opera. There is no way of knowing how Cerignola's Philharmonic played the pieces.

Sonzogno was not so much convinced by the opera as by the composer's passion for his work. Mascagni rehearsed and rehearsed («a hard task with eighty people») and met with benevolence and enthusiasm. The orchestra gave its very best and the principal singers built up the young man's self-confidence.

The triumph has already been described: «I was given sixty curtain-calls». Mascagni became a part of history, a legend and was praised to the skies.

Left, a scene from the 1947-48 production of «Cavalleria Rusticana» at Scala, with sets and costumes by Nicola Benois. Above: costume designs for Alfio, Lola (center), and Turiddu, from the first production. Top: autograph manuscript of the Intermezzo from «Cavalleria Rusticana».

13

THE PREMIERE OF «CAVALLERIA»

«Cavalleria Rusticana» at Rome's Teatro Costanzi: the «Corriere della Sera» carried a wire-service report on the morning of 16 May. «*At the Teatro Costanzi the second of the Sonzogno Competition's prize-winning operas has been performed: "Cavalleria Rusticana" by Mascagni of Leghorn, conductor of the Cerignola Philharmonic Society.*

The auditorium looked lovely. The Queen arrived and was welcomed by the royal march and applause. Giovanni Verga, Marchetti, Sgambati, and Platania were present, as were various other musicians and all the critics. Mascagni's wife and little son could be seen in a box.

The opera was a real success. The picturesque overture, during which Stagno sang from behind the curtain, had to be repeated, as did the soprano's aria, the chorus, the Intermezzo between the first and second parts, and the aria (sic) of the two women. The scene with

Left, Mascagni in Piazza Cavour, Milan; below: Franco Zeffirelli's production of «Cavalleria Rusticana» at Scala.

the glass, between Alfio and Turiddu, was enthusiastically acclaimed. The composer received twenty-three curtain-calls during the act and six at the end of the opera. The music preserves the terse power of Verga's drama».

An article in «Il Popolo Romano» testified to the opera's success and praised the prima donna, Bellincioni, and the tenor, Stagno. It went on to say: «*Mascagni can legitimately be proud of this first great victory*».
«Il Fracasso» reported that the triumph could not have been greater and that the unanimous opinion of the audience was that «Cavalleria Rusticana» is a strong, brilliant work of art. It raises high hopes for the young composer. «Don Chisciotte» reported that the performance was a triumph for Mascagni, whose wide-ranging, original work already gave proof of his artistic individuality.
The opera's Milanese premiere was reviewed as follows in the «Corriere della Sera»: «*Despite shows of enthusiasm too clamorous to have been genuine and of opposition too malicious to have been unplanned, "Cavalleria Rusticana" appears to have had a flattering success at Scala yesterday evening. It was a success that will endure and be confirmed in the evenings to come if the public manages to do without the fuss, which unfortunately has nothing to do with art... but rather with publishers' sympathies and antipathies, the influence of the performers, and even political considerations.*
....
There is no denying, however, that the applause was accorded to the best parts of the opera, while much superficial glitter that elsewhere has been taken as gold was either received in silence or greeted with open hostility. Applause greeted the prelude, which is somewhat fragmentary, and onto which Turiddu's happily conceived Siciliana is grafted. First encore. A few attempts to applaud the following chorus were stifled. Alfio's vulgar song, which had the honor of being repeated in other theaters, was not liked here, nor was the ensemble».

Mention is made of some unpleasant moments; the account then resumes as follows: «*Santuzza's sweet aria made the audience applaud again (encore)... The following scene between Santuzza and Turiddu was received in silence, as was Lola's stornello. Pantaleoni was applauded, the Alfio-Santuzza duet was not liked, and then the symphonic intermezzo caused another encore to be granted... The choral brindisi got its just desert: it was hissed. The very moving second-last scene, in which Turiddu confides in his mother... drew unanimous applause from the audience (fourth encore). After the marvelous last scene, created by Verga's genius and by the composer's tact in leaving it naked in its powerful realism, the single act ended with three curtain-calls for the performars*».
The tenor, Valere, and the soprano, Pantaleoni, were praised; the chorus was criticized as rather ugly and out of tune; and the orchestration was questioned here and there (it seemed more vacuous at Scala than to reviewers elsewhere). Seemingly put out by the work's popular vigor, the critic concluded: «A few successful musical numbers are not sufficient to justify predictions about the advent of a great opera composer or an enthusiasm that «first works» far better than this one haven't aroused. Donizetti's customery refrain springs to

JOLANDA MAGNONI

mind: See you after the second work!».
For the record, the ballet «Il Tempo» was disastrously received.

Note on the «Capobanda» («Bandmaster»). D'Annunzio's article was published in the Neapolitan newspaper «Il Mattino» on 3 September 1892. Here is the most virulent passage: «Was he, then, born to be a bandleader, as others were born to be musicians, poets, painters? So my first judgement wasn't wrong, when I saw him appear on the stage as the bestial Roman public exulted, hailing him with shouts and din».

Another of the opera's performers who helped to make Mascagni famous: Jolanda Magnoni, Santuzza at Scala during the 1950-51 season.

THE RETURN OF THE HERO

Leghorn exulted over its son's glory, with a football-club type of enthusiasm; and Cerignola, perhaps, exulted even more. Mascagni was welcomed with celebrations and fireworks, and the streets were packed beyond belief. The maestro had to enter his house by the balcony, climbing up sheets that had been knotted together. Twenty days of festivities, twenty days of superhuman happiness! Naturally, when someone has won, his one-time adversaries turn into friends and adulators.

They may even turn into greedy merchants, as was unfortunately the case with Giovanni Verga who - when he witnessed the opera's world-wide success - sued for royalties and rights of literary property. The case brought the writer 143,000 lire, a considerable sum in 1893. Verga's signature had certainly helped to attract attention to the libretto by Targioni-Tozzetti and Menasci, but one has the feeling that the opera brought greater popularity to Verga than all his short stories and novels, however beautiful they may be.

Above: Maestro Soffredini, Pietro Mascagni's teacher at Leghorn's, Luigi Cherubini Musical Institute (now named after Pietro Mascagni).
Left, a caricature by Scarpelli of the composer who, with the help of his «creations» tries to break down the door of Rome's Teatro dell'Opera, from which he had been excluded during the 1927-28 season.

PIETRO MASCAGNI, THE ITALIAN

At this point one may well ask: what, or rather who, was Pietro Mascagni? An impetuous artist, capable of portraying white-hot feelings, burning passions; a musician whose writing was genuine and quick, a natural talent who expressed himself best at difficult moments, when there was a battle to be fought.

«Cavalleria Rusticana» launched the maestro in the world of opera and brought him success; but this work conditioned the rest of his life, and not only because it remained the best, the most beautiful, and the most frequently played of his works.

This masterpiece has been called, somewhat generically, the progenitor of «verismo». The entire younger generation of Italian composers, however, knew that there was something in the air that required them to be truer and more natural - in other words, that the time for heroes had ended and the time for human beings had arrived. The works of that period that drew their inspiration from history, mythology, legends, and German romanticism had little success and were short-lived, with few exceptions. Nor was anyone successful in imitating Verdian melodrama, which, for that matter, had been abandoned even by the maestro from Busseto as early as 1871, the year of «Aida». Puccini and Giordano turned towards France for their subjects. At the same time, Italians slowly began to develop a taste for symphonic music, and the more inquisitive composers used the opportunity to improve their orchestral writing. The hearts of Italian musicians at the end of the last century were filled not only with Italian-style melody: the advent of Wagner, however late it came to Italy, and the discovery of the romantic symphony, thanks to such dedicated conductors as Martucci, automatically created a type of natural selection: those who lagged behind the times were swept away by the novelties that determined the European musical climate.

In writing «Cavalleria», Mascagni had written a very Italian opera without shutting himself up in a nationalistic cage. He had described love, jealousy, and death, and he had painted a lively portrait of a quarrelsome Sicilian environment: but he had also been able to convey a high sense of nobility in the moments preceding the catastrophe (as in Turiddu's relationship with his mother and Santuzza's confession). It is true that the choruses in «Cavalleria» are crude and not highly developed, and that the wagon-driver's song, taken on its own, is horrible.

Nevertheless, the atmosphere is right, and things are described just as they are. Remarkably, the symphonic side of Mascagni's very first works (he had been writing masses at the time) has a flavor of its own. The fashion for preludes and intermezzi, which had been

admirably advanced by Verdi himself, became a reference-point for young composers who were beginning to feel themselves strait-jacketed by the glorious old melodramatic form. This also explains Mascagni's passion (the term is not an exaggeration) for conducting. The international success of operas like «Cavalleria» and «Amico Fritz» made the composer from Leghorn leave the provinces and sniff the air of Central Europe. The world was at peace, and Italy, too - apart from its misadventures in Africa - enjoyed the benefits and experienced the social tensions; people traveled, commerce flourished, and it seemed as if mankind had found the harmony necessary for peaceful coexistentce.

Top, a caricature of Mascagni, with his autograph. Above, the Maestro with the librettista of «Cavalleria», Targioni-Tozzetti and Menasci.

SWEET «AMICO FRITZ»

Mascagni remained faithful to the publisher Sonzogno, despite Ricordi's flattery, and Sonzogno quickly realized that Mascagni's name was a goldmine. He followed the composer to Cerignola, where he had been invited to stand as godfather to Mascagni's newborn son, Edoardo. Sonzogno requested another opera; the two discussed librettists and subjects, and the idea of «L'Amico Fritz» - a German-style idyll — finally took shape. It was very different from «Cavalleria», but Mascagni wanted something new. He had no desire to stay in the southern provinces — not even in his thoughts. Thus the stage work by Erckmann and Chatrian, created in 1877 and based on a novel of the same name written in 1864, became an opera in 1891. It was completed at the publisher's home, "in the lap of luxury", as Mascagni wrote to his wife, who was far away from Milan.

In this opera Mascagni revealed the tender side of his nature. «Amico Fritz» was immediately successful, even outside Italy, but it did not have «Cavalleria Rusticana»'s staying power. Theatrically, it was rather weak; the dialogue was somewhat diffuse and the music was perhaps thinner than «Cavalleria»'s. It is more elaborate and at the same time a more classical entertainment, and it has passages of great popular appeal, such as the «Cherry Duet». But poor «Fritz» was dragged down by the reaction against «Verismo» and against «Italian» taste. In recent years it has occasionally been performed, but certainly not often enough to make it popular again.

The reviews of the first Roman performance, which again took place at the Costanzi (31 October 1891), were enthusiastic, and there were those who said that «L'Amico Fritz» was musically and conceptually much better than «Cavalleria». Cerignola had by then adopted Mascagni, but D'Annunzio's artillery took quite indecent potshots at him. The Poet's attack on the plebeian taste that provided the basis of Mascagni's support will shortly be discussed. It was an example of journalism at its worst; unfortunately, even today it has its vulgar imitators.

On this page: two productions of «L'Amico Fritz»: above, at Trieste's Teatro Verdi, 1988, below, the 1946-47 production at Scala, conducted by Antonio Guarnieri, sets by Nicola Benois.

MASCAGNI ABROAD, NEW OPERAS

The first trip abroad of the composer whom Fortune seemed to have kissed was to Vienna in 1892. Italy participated in the Imperial-Royal capital's musical exposition through its "Young School" and received incredible plaudits, in some cases greater than the worth of the works in question. To some Viennese, who lived in a tradition-oriented city, the Italian style actually seemed liberating when compared with Wagnerian ornamentation. This was understandable in a city in which the classical style and romanticism had often lived cheek-by-jowl with the emotions. Mascagni the volcano was a good representative — especially through his «Cavalleria Rusticana» - of this new, loving devotion to the South, and he received great applause and mass enthusiasm.

But Mascagni was not a man for great capitals or big cities.

The oasis of Cerignola was really sufficient for his soul, and above all, for his family. Now that he was well along in his career, and clearly not a composer merely by chance, the maestro from Leghorn presented his third opera, «I Rantzau», in Florence, where it was greeted with some hesitation on the part of the critics. The anti-Mascagni faction in the gallery, which had taken heart from D'Annunzio's violent prose (the insolent pamphlet about «The Bandmaster»), would inevitably become stronger; and the accusations of vulgarity, plebeian taste, and profanation of pure art would continue to follow Mascagni all his life, more often wrongly than rightly.

His popularity, however, was still high, and his career abroad, especially in Germany and England, continued to go well.

He disapproved of England's strait-laced customs (night life ended too early for this exuberant Mediterranean type), but he was complimented even by Queen Victoria.

Still, people began asking themselves, and with some apprehension, why «Cavalleria's» great success wasn't being repeated. Unfortunately, «I Rantzau» simply didn't work, and neither did «Guglielmo Ratcliff» which, following a long gestation-period, was premiered at La Scala in 1895; this took place shortly before the first performance of «Silvano», a short opera created to please the public.

Mascagni worked hard. The source of his creativity was virtually inexhaustible, but he ran the risk of being victimized by publishers. Be that as it may, in 1896 he became director of the Rossini Musical High School in Pesaro, a position he held dedicatedly and contentiou-

sly; and he produced another short opera, «Zanetto», which was little appreciated. He also had a preliminary contact with Ricordi for «The Japanese Woman», or «Iris».

But the most interesting item from those years may be the series of symphonic concerts he conducted at La Scala in 1898.

That year, Pietro Mascagni was principal conductor of the Orchestral Society of the Teatro alla Scala. On 22 March he conducted a «grand patriotic concert» to commemorate the «Five Days of Milan» - i.e., the heroic uprising against the Austrians. There was a great chorus of young people and the municipal band participated as well. The feverish atmosphere in the theater can easily be imagined, and the program suited the occasion: a great deal of Verdi (the overtures to «La Battaglia di Legnano» and «I Vespri Siciliani» and the chorus «O Signore dal tetto natio» from «I Lombardi»), «Suoni la tromba» (from Bellini's «I Puritani»), Mameli's Hymn (now the Italian national anthem), the overture to Rossini's «William Tell», and the Royal March and Garibaldi Hymn.

Above: the cast of the December 1951 Palermo production of «L'Amico Fritz», with Rina Malatrasi, Alvinio Misciano, the conductor Santarelli, and the baritone Vianelli.

MASCAGNI THE SYMPHONY CONDUCTOR

The «Year of Mascagni» was proceeded by a year of Campanati and followed by the advent of Arturo Toscanini. What was Mascagni like as a symphony conductor? He was certainly a conductor of temperament, capable of combining natural curiosity with a deep love of music.

Some interesting choices stand out in the programs that took place in March and April, especially when one takes into consideration the unpopularity of the symphonic genre in those days. It was deemed «foreign» - despite its three-century-old Italian history! - and not well adapted to our race.

Verdi did not like this type of musical offering, but Milan - thanks especially to the Quartet Society - had for some time thought of itself as a European city. Following the era of Italy's Reunification, Italian artists had been gazing ever more frequently beyond the Alps, and justly so, as foreign artists were gazing more and more towards Italy, too.

It is interesting that Mascagni conducted the first Italian performances of Tchaikovsky's Sixth Symphony, of Cherubini's «Medea» Overture, and of Grieg's Piano Concerto, with the pianist Ernesto Consolo. There was no lack of Wagner (excerpts from «Tristan» and «Parsifal»), and this, too, is highly indicative. There were many pieces that would today be considered «for symphonic consumption», but there were also pieces by his teachers and by other members of the Italian school - and this does honor to Mascagni.

He conducted music by Ponchielli, Buzzi-Peccia, Zuelli, Ferroni, Franchetti, Bolzoni, and even Saladino, his first teacher. The concert of 20 April 1898 was basically dedicated to contemporary (or nearly so) Italians - a sort of message based largely on novelties. Toscanini was to do something similar the following year, but for other composers. After that, Mascagni did not appear as a symphony conductor at La Scala, which justifiably became the favorite location for the greatest Italian and foreign conductors, and which directed its sights towards a different concept of the art of music. But the composer of «Cavalleria Rusticana» continued to conduct his operas at La Scala, on various fortunate occasions.

On this page, two models for the world premiere (1898) of «Iris» at Rome's Teatro Costanzi, conducted by Mascagni himself after he had fought with Edoardo Mascheroni, who had originally been given the job of conducting the opera.

IRIS,
THE EXOTIC
FLOWER

LA BELLEZZA

MUSICANTE

«Iris», the first opera Mascagni wrote for Ricordi, had its first performance on 22 November 1898 at Rome's Teatro Costanzi, which had become a sort of feudal fortress for Mascagni. As has already been said, the opera had a Japanese setting. It was a popular success at its opening, but critical opinion was divided. Having clashed with the principal conductor, Edoardo Mascheroni, the composer himself conducted the new work. It is remarkable that Mascagni dared approach an exotic, Liberty-style subject, and that this happened before Puccini described the Japan of «Butterfly» and of Captain Pinkerton (1904).

Mascagni, like Puccini, studied Japanese instruments (at a museum in Fiesole) and was enchanted with their sounds - so new to a Mediterranean ear. But Mascagni's interest in the exotic did not go much further than that. Luigi Illica's libretto tells a somewhat grim tale, worthy of the old Oriental «bandit» novels. The story of poor Iris, who is mistreated, kidnapped, and humiliated, and who makes up her mind to die - she even comes close to being eaten by jackals - is much less fascinating than that of the equally unfortunate Cio-Cio-San. «Iris», however, was one of the young Mascagni's favorite operas, in part because of several admirable passages, such as the Hymn to the Sun (conterpart of the Humming Chorus in «Butterfly»).

It was no joke, however, to have Giacomo Puccini ta-

king your path. The maestro from Lucca was unarguably of greater stature than Mascagni, and he had the advantage of coming from a cultured family. Above all, he had a magical sense of theater. The dramatic aspect of Puccini's work is always impeccable; Mascagni's is hardly ever so. Like Puccini, Mascagni had an enormous melodic gift, but he proceeded by fits and starts, and more by instinct than by intention. The differences between the two composers were already clear when they were at the Milan Conservatory, and in time they became accentuated. Mascagni lived much longer than Puccini, who was unable to bring his artistic parabola to a close; but Mascagni, a good decade before his death, has already said all he had to say, and he felt cut out or passed over, despite the Academician's cocked-hat he was given to wear.

Above: two costumes for the world premiere of Mascagni's «Japanese» opera. Below right: a poster for the world premiere (1898) of «Iris»; left: the set for «Iris» at the Teatro dei Pupi (Puppet Theater), Leghorn, summer 1988.

«CAVALLERIA» AND NATIONALISM

Puccini remains the real protagonist of that period. His «Bohème» annihilated Leoncavallo's and «Butterfly» somehow buried «Iris».

But the unhappy heroine in Liberty-style (in a manner of speaking - and indeed the style of the score's cover shouts it out) had at least one positive outcome: a reconciliation with D'Annunzio. It would be equally legitimate, however, to assume that this «rapprochement», which would culminate in a joint work («Parisina»), confirmed the Poet's bad taste: he conveived of art as a sort of refined get-up, and he did not understand that Mascagni's strong points were to be found - still and always - in «Cavalleria's big, warm heart.

«Il Tempo» published an ample coverage of the first performance of «Iris» at La Scala, replete with drawings and caricatures. The evening was reported and reviewed in minute detail: the end of the prelude was encored, and so was Johr's song, sung by De Lucia. After that, according to the reporter, the atmosphere grew chillier. During the scene with the puppets, someone shouted: «*We're at the Girolamo*», which was Milan's historic marionette theater (now closed).

IRIS

MUSICA DI P. MASCAGNI
LIBRETTO DI L. ILLICA
G. RICORDI & C. EDITORI

OFFICINE G. RICORDI & C. MILANO

A Liberty-style poster for Mascagni's «Iris». Below, a scene from Scala's 1987 production of «Madama Butterfly», which won that year's Abbiati Prize. This opera has always been one of «Iris»'s competitors. Next page: a traditional pair at Scala - «Cavalleria» and «Pagliacci» - the former with Ghena Dimitrova (Santuzza), the latter with Josè Carreras (Canio) and John Rawnsley (Tonio).

People were arguing in the foyer: «*It's beautiful*». «*What is?*», «*The Hymm to the Sun*». «*And the rest?*», «*We'll see*». There were even a few small protests at the end of the second act, and there were few curtain-calls at the very end, which proved that the opera had been only half successful.

Unfortunately, even among the most benevolent commentators, Mascagni's name remained and would always remain bound up with his first opera. One says: the composer of «Cavalleria»; everything was compared to «Cavalleria», and someone was always sure to call every new work «Cavalleria translated into another language» - Japanese, in this case. For Mascagni, it was a subtle, perfidious form of persecution; he continued to change his style, but never completely succeeded.

For that matter, this was one of the tragedies of Italian music, which did not manage to claim its rightful place in Europe until after World War II - after all the good and bad rhetoric of the past had been thoroughly digested. This rhetoric produced a whole series of shams, from false medieval style to false renaissance style, not to mention the decadence that set itself up in opposition to the grim culture of fascism.

The reasons underlying this cultural tragedy may be summed up in a few words: the desire to become part of Europe was undermined in the first place by an ill-conceived form of nationalism (being Italian was the main thing), in the second by public taste and the taste of the regime, and finally by lower and middle-class traditions. Italian culture was rooted in melodrama and was therefore inclined to oversimplify; and the cult of «verismo» (understood as the use of a common language) only aggravated the situation.

Many operas of the Young Italian School demonstra-

te a desire to escape: French- or German-style orchestral writing, a bit of «Carmen» and a bit of Wagner, with the ancient declamatory style prevailing over full-throated singing. But sooner or later, all our composers found themselves recrossing the river - and lo and behold, there was the barrel-chested, swollen-lunged tenor dominating the stage once again.

The performances, too, were influenced by this atmosphere, and the composers themselves were sometimes accomplices: when they conducted, they «threw themselves in whole-heartedly», and the result was like a mob-scene in a piazza. Mascagni, too, paid a price for this continuous betrayal of Verdi's «measuredness». If it is possible, today, to listen more respectfully to «Iris» than it was in its own day, this is because interpretive civility has improved. One can now discover, in this sea of music, a number of islands that do more honor to the composer than any tenor's shouting could possibly do.

Puccini alone thoroughly understood the system. He had at his command an immense melodic gift (worthy of the appellation «High Art») and an infallible sense of theater, so that he was able to approach French and American subjects with a sure hand and to become truly international. His success was not fortuitous. To recount even a cruel story, as in «Il Tabarro», he turned to Paris; and his tribute to high Renaissance «Florentinism» was carried out with total irony, in «Gianni Schicchi». No one would deny that Puccini was «Italian», but he was a modern Italian with European tastes. Had he lived another twenty years, he might have cast off towards other shores rather than turning back, defeated, from «Turandot's» beaches.

Puccini followed a plan (with outstanding commercial acumen, we might add) that was destined to make him into a universal artist, whereas Mascagni, who was much more choleric and illogical, jumped from one temptation to another and ended up by being inconsistent. As Mascagni never managed to become an aesthete, poet, minstrel, or tale-spinner, Verga's novel remained his indelible, ineradicable label as well as his lifebuoy for the whole of his life. «You know, oh mother». «I know the fault is mine». «Heeeyyy! They're killed our Turiddu!».

A scene from Puccini's «Il Tabarro», which was performed along with «Cavalleria» at the Puccini Festival at Torre del Lago; this photo is of Scala's 1986-87 production with Giovanna Casolla (Giorgetta) and Eleonora Jankovic (La Frugola).

LE MASCHERE

In 1901, at a time of big personal commitments, when he was at the apogee of success, Mascagni virtually challenged all of Italy with «Le Maschere».

Published by Sonzogno, «Le Maschere» is an Italian-style opera with a touch of «commedia dell'arte», which had never gone completely out of fashion in Italy. With Luigi Illica's help, Mascagni tried to resuscitate this national glory; it was an excellent idea that Puccini would not reject some years later and that was used even by Ferruccio Busoni. As on so many other occasions, however, Mascagni's intuition often put him in the vanguard, but he lacked the refinement and balance to realize his goals.

«Le Maschere» was launched as one of the most important new works of the year. It opened simultaneously in six cities: in Rome with the composer on the podium, and in Milan, Venice, Turin, Genoa, and Verona. For technical reasons, a seventh city, Naples, only saw the opera two days after the fateful 17th of January.

What was the outcome? In Rome the performance went well, or at least reasonably well, thanks in part to the composer's presence, but elsewhere the opera was booed. This led immediately to cuts and changes, insertions and improvements; but the opera was to remain an ambiguous work, what with its combining of 18th-century love interest and popular, operetta-like effects. With all its jokes, rambling speeches, and perfumed tenderness, in the end «Le Maschere» satisfied no one.

On this page: two scenes from «Le Maschere»: above, Angelo Romero (Capitan Spaventa) and Giuseppe Sabbatini (Arlecchino), in a production at Ravenna in Festival, remounted in Bologna during the 1988-89 season; left, another scene from the same production.

25

MASCAGNI, THE FIERY PODIUM

Mascagni was much esteemed as a conductor, even in the symphonic repertoire. He was invited to Russia, where he conducted Tchaikovsky's «Pathétique» Symphony with heart-rending fervor, but he was deeply depressed by the way of life he observed there and by the social injustice that divided the country into «masters and slaves». For that matter, Mascagni - a good Italian accustomed to home-grown pleasures - never showed much curiosity about foreign countries. This became clear during an American tour that was fraught with successes and disappointments and marred by the abominable tricks of foul-playing, dishonest impresarios. Whether it was real or sham, Mascagni's homesickness assumed characteristics we all know: he felt alone and unhappy when he was away from home and family, and this despite the fact that his native Leghorn was a city of sailors.

But Mascagni was liked by the Germans and other northerners. Gustav Mahler, who was certainly poles apart from him artistically, held him in high regard and invited him to Vienna. He found in Mascagni that Mediterranean heat and fervor which functioned as a counterbalance to what some considered Wagnerian heaviness. Even the severe critic Hanslick thought highly of Mascagni. Was this the illusion of artists looking for strong emotions? A return to the noble savage? Let's not go too far. Nevertheless, Mascagni was certainly not a run-of-the-mill person: he had temperament, a love of sound, and a great desire to understand others. As is always the case with our compatriots, his instincts helped him to overcome the gaps in his knowledge. Those who saw Mascagni on the podium before World War II will certainly remember his highly informal appearance - a vision brought forward from the end of the last century to the less than radiant days of the fascist regime.

On the podium, Mascagni demonstrated the same vehemence that he had shown during his sometimes tempestuous directorship of the Rossini High School in Pesaro and as the artistic director of Rome's Teatro Costanzi. (He assumed this position in 1909, and it should be noted that his first season opened with «Tristan und Isolde»: Wagner was being supported by an Italian of a totally different cultural background.

Had psychoanalysis been heard of in Italy at that time, Mascagni would have ended up on a couch, confessing his weaknesss and complexes. «I don't want to be what I was», he would have said. «Save me from this all-pervasive father» - Verga - «and get Santuzza, Lola, Alfio, and Turiddu out of my sight. I hate them, I even dream of them at night, they are bad and overbearing. Save me, Professor, from the best part of my own ego.»

On these pages: posters, postcards, calendars, and caricatures related to Mascagni and his operas.
Left: a calendar with «Parisina»; below, right: playbill for an orchestral tour with Mascagni; left: a calendar with «Le Maschere».
On the page to the right: a playbill for the 1895-96 Carnival season in Ferrara, with «I Rantzau» on the program; from top to bottom: a caricature of Mascagni as conductor; an engraving of a scene from «I Rantzau», from the world premiere, which took place in Florence, frontispiece of the libretto of «Cavalleria» as it was presented to the Sonzogno Competition.

FROM «AMICA» TO «ISABEAU»

Left: Piero Schiavazzi (Giorgio) and Elena Bianchini Cappelli (Amica), protagonists of the first production (1905) of Mascagni's opera «Amica». Below, a scene from the world premiere of «Isabeau» in 1912.

The professor would have advised Mascagni to look for another father and to try out the game of repentance and forgiveness. In fact, Mascagni did find and try out an antidote called D'Annunzio: he worked with the very same poet who had been calling him a bandmaster - and a circus bandmaster at that.

But Pietro Mascagni was a fertile composer, always

looking for something new and different.

«Amica's» source is French - the libretto was taken from Choudens - and it is a tragedy painted in primary colors. Its first performance took place at Monte Carlo in 1905. It is richly orchestrated, and some called it a compromise with Wagnerism - an illness that some people thought should never touch a real Italian. Torn between two lovers, Amica ends up in a ravine during a terrible storm. The singers shout and the orchestra shouts; and «Amica» was not a lucky work.

«Isabeau», which had its premiere at Buenos Aires in 1911 after a festive preview in Genoa, is a more complicated and interesting work. Mascagni's new-found aestheticism (although Mascagni was anything but an aesthete) had hints of the antique and even of the erotic in it. Isabeau, in fact, was based on the British legend of Lady Godiva, who was forced to ride on horseback clad only in her hair - naked, in other words.

«Isabeau» is a work of Italian-style decadence, which was nourished on ancient memories and on the illusion that once upon a time there were beauty and honor, and heroes flourished. It was one of a host of flights from reality, in which love and mysticism could be combined in a sort of sanctification. «Isabeau» also con-

Above: a poster for «Isabeau» (1912). Right: Amero Cagnoni's portrait of Luigi Illica, the librettist of «Isabeau». Left: a contemporary postcard inspired by the protagonists of «Amica».

tains the notion of the forbidden fruit and of innocence that must never be violated: Isabeau naked on horseback is perhaps the incarnation of desire. But the young princess is bold as well as angelic. When the unknown youth, Folco, who ought not to have looked at her but has looked all the same, is captured through trickery and then condemned, the girl feels somehow guilty; as she cannot save him, she decides to die with him. Folco is blinded but happy because he has captured the Image - the one thing that time can never destroy. This ultra-refined little touch is very D'Annunzian.

Was the poet fascinated with «Isabeau» because he himself was a voyeur, a peeping Tom? Or was he not perhaps seduced by an opera in which there are no set-pieces (at least according to Mascagni), and in which the composer is always ready to cross the Rubicon, always thinking of Wagner, Strauss, and Debussy - even if he always turns back at the last minute. Mascagni refined his harmonies, invented clearer skies, and chased the shades of Alfio and Turiddu far away; but he was still tempted to go for violent or tragic endings. (One can almost hear: They've killed our Folco!) The nightmare continued, even if the characters in «Isabeau» bore historic names and were apparently cultivated (and, all in all, rather comical).

Mascagni thought he had made a profession of faith in Italian romanticism; but a long time had already elapsed since the days of the national-popular plans that had stirred the spirits of the citizenry during the Reunification. «Isabeaus'» Liberty-style romanticism, with its Randolfo da Dublinos and its Ermyntrudes and Ermyngardes, ended up as nothing more than the precursor of the cloak-and-dagger films that paralyzed much of Italian cinema up to the 1940s.

It is amusing to note that Isabeau, a somewhat frigid princess, not inclined to marry, and forced into a contest with her suitors, became a sort of cousin to Turandot - not in a mythical Peking, but amidst stereotypical medieval tombs and papier-maché.

Above, Gabriele D'Annunzio (called Il Vate - The Bard). Right: the Teatro Colon in Buenos Aires, where the first performance of «Isabeau» was given. On the following pages: above, left: a chromolithograph by Gaetano Previati dipicting the first act of «Parisina»; below, Plinio Nomellini's poster for «Parisina» (1913).

D'ANNUNZIO, MASCAGNI, AND «LA PARISINA»

Who would ever have guessed that Mascagni and D'Annunzio would have ended up writing an opera together? Careless D'Annunzian critics hardly ever mention «La Parisina», preferring rather to discuss «The Martyrdom of St. Sebastian» that he collaborated on with Debussy or his work with Ildebrando Pizzetti. Yet it's a fact: the crude musician from Leghorn and the super-refined poet from Pescara set sail together to-

wards distant shores - shores that were seemingly off-limits to Italian opera composers. Since the days of «Iris», Gabriele D'Annunzio thought he had discovered something new in Mascagni and had taken back his venomous attacks on «the Bandmaster». Perhaps he was attracted to a Real Italian, who might perhaps have been capable of bringing a breath of the heroic present into the splendors of early Renaissance courts and culture.

The pose was a bit of a falsifier in everything he did: he was a convinced formalist, a literary snob, an Anglo-French-style romantic decadent, and a man of action who combined bedroom pleasures with the voluptuousness of believing himself destined for heroism and myth. The story of Parisina and Ugo takes place amidst licit and illicit love, planned and postponed encounters, agitation and melancholy. The atmosphere is the same as that of the myriad versions of Paolo and Francesca da Rimini, with a touch of Byronism thrown is for good measure.

The most amusing aspect of the matter is that Mascagni, who wasn't the least bit intimidated by his new partner, readily absorbed his snobbery. For the baker's son, the poet who called himself The Image-Maker was nothing other than a man with whom it was useful to work. The maestro had not even been impressed by the Americans, whom he had defined (with a few exceptions) as "men like any others". Can we, then, imagine D'Annunzio a bit irritated, a bit uneasy in the throes of this work?

The poet who believed above all in his poetry, and the composer who had to bend the poetry to the music's requirements, both worked in unaccustomed ways — and in Paris, at that. For Mascagni it was a matter of finding a special modus operandi, as D'Annunzio's text was certainly anti-operatic, if not downright anti-theatrical. To create an Italian «Tristan» was enormously risky, because there would have been nothing in it that was like either «Tristan» or Italy.

The premiere of this grandiose, endless opera took place at La Scala in Milan on 15 december 1913, before a distinguished audience. The performance began at 8.30 p.m. and went on until nearly 2 a.m. - which did not cheer the hearts of the worshippers of rapid, immediate, Italian-style drama; its dimensions, therefore, were indeed «Tristan»-like. It had been sublimely packaged (even the libretto had been illustrated by the painter Previati), for whenever D'Annunzio did anything the world rushed to be present, and art and high society joined hands. In short, it was an event. But the idea of combining words and music in a new language ran up against the total verbosity of a text that was anything but modern. Those were times, however, of great abstract adventures, at least in theory; in reality, the cannon salesmen were preparing a true piece of «verismo»: a realistic war that was to bring troubles to artists who - D'Annunzio excepted - were not particularly gifted in that area.

The long opera immediately underwent amputations. Mascagni was much more expert than the poet and understood that the scissors had to be wielded if the opera was to be saved. This he did, thereby saddening D'Annunzio.

For that matter, D'Annunzio's fluent language required an equally fluent current of sound. Mascagni had

dedicated five months to the orchestration of «Parisina» which, moreover, was a great inspiration to Plinio Nomellini, who created the flower-bedecked, Liberty-style poster for the production. The scoring was carried out with tenacity but also with fear - fear of words, obviously. Courtly language indeed! For Mascagni, love and fury are one and the same, violence is expressed in roars; let the poet say what he will: here we've reached the limit of feeling. Beyond this point lies either obsession or madness.

Was it worth the effort? Judging by the opera's fortunes, one would have to say it wasn't. Still, it is clear that after the premiere Mascagni was no longer afraid of his librettist and that, on the contrary, he was beginning to take deep breaths and to huff and puff. He had realized that only a Wagner may exceed an average listening time; therefore, with the consent of the librettist, who seemed to be distancing himself from his creation, Mascagni wielded the hatchet.

In vain. The fourth act was removed, as were the scene in which Parisina reads about Paolo and Francesca and various other musical pieces, but the opera never took hold. Mascagni's encounter with D'Annunzio did neither of them any good. In reality, to succeed in tandem with D'Annunzio one had either to be like him or to submit to him. Other composers fared better than Mascagni, but they did not manage to make an important new contribution to our operatic and theatrical tradition.

Gabriele D'Annunzio working with Alberto Franchetti on «La Figlia di Iorio». Mascagni's «Isabeau» was also a setting of a text by D'Annunzio. Other composers who drew inspiration from the poet included Zandonai, Montemezzi, and Pizzetti.

FROM «LODOLETTA» TO «IL PICCOLO MARAT»

The war came. Mascagni was not enthusiastic about it: he said that wars produce hatred and make everything lose ground. He seemed to be moderately sympathetic to socialism at that time. He wrote the opera «Lodoletta», first produced at the Costanzi in Rome in 1917, and the operetta «Sì»; neither of them added anything to the maestro's reputation. Then, in 1919, he completed «Il Piccolo Marat». Giovacchino Forzano's libretto was based on the French Revolution, the Convention, the Terror, and so on. Whose side did it take? Therein lies the problem. Robespierre, queens, and politicians did not appear on stage («Do you think it will be possible», asked Mascagni, «to make Lenin sing a century from now?''), and it seemed a better idea to treat the facts of the story through the eyes of normal people. In so doing, however, Mascagni — who may have been disappointed with the results of his experiments with new techniques — took a step backwards. He tried to rejuvenate himself by returning to the style of «Cavalleria» and, to some extent, of «Fritz». But it was too late. In «Marat», revolutionary furor becomes grotesque. The composer unfurled flags in the breeze and went back to shouting; he freed himself from ornamentation and culture and again offered the public a brightly-colored popular drama, made to please all those who demanded that art be both morality and consolation.

The fate of eternally occupying second place was almost

a curse on Mascagni. «Il Piccolo Marat» was crushed by Giordano's «Andrea Chénier», which remained in the repertoire — in part because it contains the seeds of doubt. Mascagni hewed out his work with an axe, eschewing nuances; and he killed his second-last opera. The maestro was nevertheless destined to be swallowed up by the fascist regime's nationalism: he was to be the flag-bearer of the nation's spirit, he was to be hono-

Left, a publicity postcard for «Lodoletta». Right: the libretto of «Sì», Mascagni's only operetta, written in collaboration with Carlo Lombardo. Below left, the composer with the cast of «Lodoletta» (1917).

red and esteemed. Have him conduct some of the operas he wrote when he was young and we'll make him a member of the Academy.

When it was first performed in May 1921 «Il Piccolo Marat» seemed to be a patriotic opera, capable of arousing political enthusiasm (Mascagni the «Leftist» was liked first by the nationalists and then by the fascists); later, however, doubts were expressed. The subject was said to be worthy of «Les Miserables» or of the worst anti-Jacobin tales, but it was treated with sympathy vis-à-vis the Idea. A few pages were insufficient to insure a stage life for «Il Piccolo Marat», whereas they were sufficient to make «Chénier» immortal. Nor was it a good idea to use the word «Piccolo»: when Victor Hugo called Napoleon III «le Petit» the latter's image was destroyed in France.

Left, Rosina Storchio, the first Lodoletta, at Rome's Teatro Costanzi, 30 April 1917. Below and left: two scenes from the world premiere of «Il Piccolo Marat», which took place at the Teatro Costanzi on 2 May 1921.

THE LAST OPERA: NERONE

The composer was to remain in creative hibernation until 1935. He conducted, he became public figure, and he was to all outward appearances a model of good behavior in respect to Italian culture. He is said to have been a reactionary, an enemy of jazz, and, later, an embittered man - rather like the much more dangerous D'Annunzio, who had been put to pasture at Gardone. The government gave Mascagni tasks and honors and sent him to congresses, but it was not pleased when Mascagni protested, created a ruckus, or complained about abuses of power or of inefficiency. In politics, too, he was eternally Number Two, inasmuch as he was made a member of the Academy, whereas Puccini had been given a senatorship. Like most other members of the middle class, Mascagni supported fascism; he was fascinated by Mussolini, who was a music lover and who used rhetoric in the manner of a tenor. To break the impasse, the composer ought to have become more cunning, but how can one demand that an old Tuscan from

On this page, items relating to Mascagni's last opera, «Nerone». To the left: the first page of the autograph manuscript of the score. Below, left: Aureliano Pertile, who sang the title role at the world premiere on 16 January 1935. Below: Mascagni receives the cast's congratulations.

Leghorn learn the subtle art of slyness?

With his unruly forelock always flying around when he was on the podium, Pietro Mascagni never even managed to become the regime's official composer - and that is to his credit. He was rich and famous, but that wasn't enough: he continued to feel more and more alienated. The once handsome youth had become heavy-set; the caricaturists did not treat him nicely; his face had become a grim mask. The photo of him in his Academician's uniform is unintentionally funny: he looks like an old actor.

In setting to work on «Nerone», the story of the Roman emperor, could the maestro have been identifying with the collapse of Roman civilization and with the abject life of the arsonist-tyrant? Perhaps he could have. Fascist criticism seems to have been perplexed by his choice of so negative a character at a time when everyone was praising Caesar and when the word Dux, Duce, was written on every wall. It is well known that the people of Leghorn have difficult personalities, and perhaps this was how Mascagni, old Leghornian that he was, viewed the concept of «Roman-ness» and those who believed in it: it was the kingdom of vice, of excessive power, of cowardliness, and the exaltation of the killer. Nerone, dramatic and bloody, enemy of the

PIETRO MASCAGNI

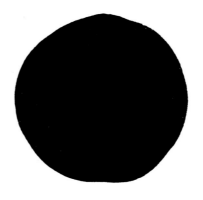

NERONE

Left: the first printed libretto of the opera «Nerone». Below, Edoardo Marchioro's model for one of the opera's scenes. On the following pages: above, a poster for the first performance at Bologna's Teatro Comunale (7 November 1924) of Boito's «Nerone»; below, Giuseppe Noto (Petronio) and Lina Bruna Rasa (Atte) at the first performance of Mascagni's opera in 1935.

Christians (if possible, after the Concordate), and an arsonist for pleasure. Didn't the nation's history offer anything better? asked Marco Ramperti in «La Stampa». But how can Caesar be made to sing? Officially, Mascagni flirted with fascism and offered every possible type of flattery; but perhaps, deep down inside, he detested it. This is not a new idea, but it is an attractive one. «Nerone» was not liked, although the old maestro's work gained respect. Franco Abbiati wrote a long review of it for the «Corriere della Sera» of 17 January 1935. It bore the headline: «*The premiere of Mascagni's "Nerone" at La Scala*»; and the sub-headline read: «*An audience of exceptional size and distinction proclaims the opera a great success*». A news report speaks of an unforgettable evening and of the Duce's interest in the work, although he was not present at the performance. A few illuminating phrases are to be found in the review, which was only formally under the regime's control.

«*The success of the first production of "Nerone" was a forgone conclusion, but the intensity and honesty of the reception have few precedents. Nero was many-sided and elusive, and his life has been made to seem repugnant, almost inconceivable, as a result of the infinitely thick crust of literary, historic, and legendary interpretations that have transformed it over the centuries. These factors could lead listeners to an ill-considered or even invalid "a priori" judgement, based purely on personal convictions. It is even more obvious that this "Nerone" - as conceived by Cossa, reelaborated by Targioni-Tozzetti, and set to music by Mascagni - could create a rather surprising and disorienting impression here and there. But every once in awhile, the Maestro has struck his own personal chord of passion and of lyric sentimentality, and has shown his ability to approach us, fascinate us, and convince us with this opera as with those of the past, and to open with ease a path to our hearts. There were six curtain-calls for the artists after the first act, and lively approval was demonstrated towards Mascagni. There were nine others after the second — seven of which were directed at Mascagni and the artists and two for the Maestro alone — and nine more after the third, divided exactly as after the second. This does not take into account the frequent bursts of applause during the performance. All this confirms that the magnificent event was an irresistible success, and it had opened with a unanimous ovation for the composer when he climbed onto the podium, and with the joyfully welcomed performance of the national Anthems.*

«*... In our opinion, the authentic "deus ex machina" of this musical drama is the restraining Atte, a freed-woman: from a dramatic point of view, she is the best delineated character in the opera. But the most sensitive nucleus of Mascagni's warm and copious inspiration is undoubtedly represented by the amorous palpitations of little, sacrificed Egloge; the composer's most persuasive and sincere passages are given to her. The piece's emotions run the gamut from base eroticism to*

stoical sacrifice, but the love that reigns supreme is the only sentiment that leaves a convincing imprint on the characters... Neither the excitable, voluble artist-emperor nor the masses of players, athletes, freedmen, senators, and clowns who surround the stolid protagonist, each with his own aim in view, ever reach the same level of importance - not because this spiritually murky, confused world seems inert, but simply because of these characters' operatic inconsistency.

«As to the Roman-ness of the subject, it has already been stated that this was probably not one of the Maestro's preoccupations. In fact, the Roman atmosphere is saturated with greatness and power only in the last scene, when Nero's death is represented (musically, too) in a way that is sorrowful and desolate but also plastic and solemn; thus, for an instant, it synthesizes the elements that presumably drive the plot: thirst for glory and voluptuousness, Roman majesty, art's vanity, and the inexorability of the destiny for which the emperor's horrible comet marked him. Mascagni has delineated these elements in a few passages in the first two acts:

in Nevio's declamation, inveighing against the decadence of the Empire and proclaiming the advent of Christ's law; in the hymn of the praetorian guards in Rome; in Atte's generous exhortations; and in the Dionysian chorus and tempestuous interlude of Act III, in which the most resounding sonorities are piled one on top of another and then gradually softened into a feeble, sad lament as the curtain opens on the Roman campagna.

«Regarding the choice of expressive means to be used in "Nerone", it must be said that the Maestro has applied the same criteria as in all his previous works. This opera seems to be better coordinated and more organic than its predecessors, but it is bound up with them by virtue of the pre-eminence of its vocality, its linear structure, and its melodic and harmonic pacing, which vaguely recall the idyllic "Fritz", the vehement "Ratcliff", the solar "Iris", and the carefree "Maschere". The diaphonic system is confirmed here even more decisively than in the earlier operas, and this may indicate that the composer intended to Romanize his musical linguistic style...»

Below: the composer with his grandson, Pietro. Next page: the Maestro at the Arena di Verona and (below) a telegram from Costanzo Ciano, for the fortieth anniversary of «Cavalleria».

HIS LAST YEARS

Mascagni dedicated his last years mainly to conducting. He didn't stop even when his legs would no longer hold him up and when he had to be helped to the podium. He knew that this was his last bond with music and with the people who continued to love him. When Mascagni was nearly eighty he conducted important recorded versions of «Cavalleria Rusticana» and «L'Amico Fritz».

The maestro lived in a hotel, although he owned homes of his own. His last ideals collapsed: Mussolini behaved like one of the latter, minor Roman emperors, and the anti-fascists considered Mascagni to be one of the regime's left-overs. It is said that before he died, he had a conversation with his last creation, «Nerone». To die on 2 August 1945 was a nasty business for the old idol of opera-lovers: people had other things to think about, and some were probably amazed to learn that he had survived that long.

But the composer of «Cavalleria» is still alive, nearly half a century later. He is honored and remembered. Even his less fortunate works are being revived, in a new spirit and with a new sort of attention to their musical values. Today, even young people can get to know nearly all of Mascagni's output, which disappeared so quickly from playbills and from the repertoire. From «Le Maschere» to «Il Piccolo Marat», from «L'Amico Fritz» to «Parisina», a quiet revival is taking place, and it is happening out of love for an artist who, all in all, was unhappy and unfortunate despite his success and despite his glory.

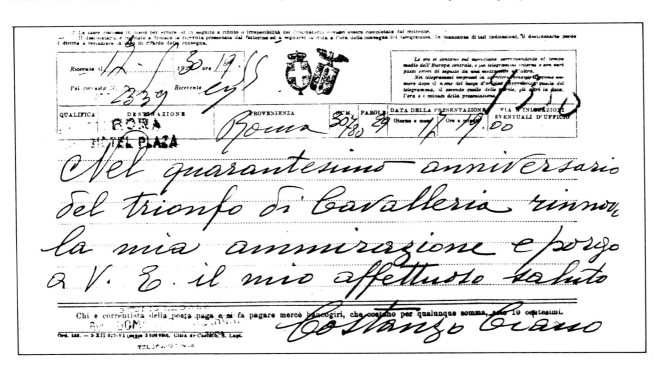

MASCAGNI IN THE NEW WORLD

by John W. Freeman

Unlike his friend and rival Giacomo Puccini, Mascagni never had a world premiere at the Metropolitan Opera, nor did he ever come to the Met to see an opera of his prepared. His only experience with North America was a fairly disastrous tour undertaken in 1902/03, which he referred to ruefully as «un sacco di guai» - a pack of troubles. These troubles started when the composer, at the height of his fame and not quite thirty-nine years of age, decided or was persuaded to form a touring company with which to barnstorm to the New World. Touring opera and theater troupes, today an ever decreasing economic possibility, were at

the time the lifeblood of the performing arts on the huge American Continent, there being of course no radio at the time and only a few records.

Part of the troupe assembled for this enterprise never succeeded in leaving Italy. Those who did were detained at Ellis Island because of a dispute over work permits. The matter was settled by compromise, whereby Mascagni had to hire some local musicians, but he feared saboteurs among them. The original plan called for 100 performances in fifteen weeks, coast to coast. This goal was never realized; while the time period eventually stretched out to six months, performances of the trou-

Above: two of the performers in the most recent American revival of «Lodoletta», Alan Held and Maria Spacagna at the New Jersey Opera House in 1989.
Left: Richard Tucker looks defiant in the role of Turiddu

On the previous page, the composer in San Francisco (above), and a scene from a 1951 production of «Cavalleria Rusticana» with Richard Tucker (Turiddu) and Zinka Milanov (Santuzza). To the left: the facade of the Metropolitan Opera House in 1908

pe never got beyond Chicago. Though Mascagni himself continued to California, where he enjoyed acclaim as a guest conductor of concerts. For the failure of the tour he blamed greedy and opportunistic managers. For their part, they blamed Mascagni for capricious, temperamental behavior, a cavalier attitude toward money and a poor organizational sense. There seems to have been justification on both sides, as well as a plethora of irresponsible charges and several lawsuits, eventually settled to no one's clear satisfaction.

Under the circumstances, it is more remarkable that the tour enjoyed such an artistic success. Poorly organized and managed though it surely was, it found appreciative audiences and critics in most of the cities visited - Boston, Springfield, Providence, Syracuse, Scranton, Detroit, Indianapolis and others in the U.S., as well as the Canadian centers of Montreal and Toronto. The chief offering was Mascagni's travelling production of «Cavalleria Rusticana», usually preceded by a concert of music by various composers, culminating in the Hymn to the Sun from Mascagni's «Iris». The latter opera was presented onstage in Philadelphia (October 14, 1902) and New York (October 16) for the first times in America.

His earlier «Guglielmo Ratcliff», another promised American premiere, never materialized, because Mascagni felt the production was not in presentable shape. Soloists on the tour included only two fairly well-known names, Eugenia Mantelli (who joined the company in New York) and Antonio Paoli, the Puerto Rican te-

On these last pages: two productions of «Cavalleria Rusticana» in the United States. Left: Julian Patrick (Compar Alfio). Below:, from left to right, John Alexander (Turiddu), Muriel Greenspon (Mamma Lucia), Frances Junger (Lola), at Houston Opera House.

nor. Elena Bianchini-Cappelli, was one of the Santuzzas. Other singers included baritone Virgilio Bellati, Dora De Filippe, Josephine Del Parto, Maria Farneti, Menotti Frascona, bass Francesco Navarini and tenor Pietro Schiavazzi, Though the company broke up in Chicago early in 1903 and most of its members returned home, Mascagni, buoyed by public enthusiasm, particularly from the Italo-American communities in various cities, hoped to rally new forces for a Cuban tour. The plan fell through, and on April 2 he and his wife embarked for Italy. Despite his harrowing experiences, Mascagni professed to have liked America and declared he would return in the fall. He never did. It would remain for «Cavalleria rusticana» almost alone to keep his fame alive.

«Cavalleria rusticana» had been a hit in America since its debut at the Philadelphia Grand Opera on September 9, 1891, and has remained so to this day. Most opera companies in the U.S. have presented it, but the focus of attention falls on the Metropolitan Opera, because of that company's longstanding international status. The Met premiere of «Cavalleria» took place on December 30, 1891, not quite four months after the U.S. premiere in Philadelphia, and the work has been present for most Met seasons since then.

The first cast included Emma Eames as Santuzza and Fernando Valero as Turiddu, with Auguste Vianesi conducting. (His name was properly «Augusto», but in New York he used the French spelling). It was a number of years, however, before «Cavalleria» formed its

Two productions of «Cavalleria» at the Metropolitan. Above, Giulietta Simionato (Santuzza) and Frank Valentino (Compar Alfio) in 1960.
Left, Grace Bumbry (Santuzza) and Carlotta Ordassy (Mamma Lucia).
On the next page, Muriel Greenspon (Mamma Lucia) and Anena Lampropoulos (Santuzza) at the Houston Opera House.

permanent liaison with Leoncavallo's «Pagliacci» as a surefire double bill. Through the first decade of the twentieth century, «Cavalleria» was paired with a variety of other operas-Gluck's «Orfeo ed Euridice» (for the premiere), Gounod's «Philémon et Baucis» (for Emma Calvé's first Santuzza in 1893), Act II of Mascagni's own «L'Amico Fritz», acts from «Carmen» or «La Traviata», cut versions of «Lucia di Lammermoor» or «Don Pasquale», and so on. «Pagliacci» too was an occasional partner- sometimes preceding, sometimes following-but when Arturo Toscanini took over as principal conductor in 1908, he chose the American premiere of Puccini's «Le Villi» to complete the double bill.

The Santuzza of Toscanini's choice, Emmy Destinn, eventually proved to be one of the most frequent exponents of the role in Met history, singing it almost forty times. In this she was surpassed only by Calvé and Zinka Milanov, with Rosa Ponselle very close behind. Other frequent Santuzzas with the company have been Johanna Gadski (Toscanini's second choice), Maria Jeritza, Florence Easton, Grace Bumbry and Fiorenza Cossotto.

And quite a number of eminent sopranos, from Celestina Boninsegna, Elisabeth Rethberg and Claudia Muzio to Gina Cigna, Cloe Elmo and Giulietta Simionato, sang one or a few performances of this role.

Among the Met's exponents of Turiddu, nearly all have also sung Canio in «Pagliacci», though not necessarily at the same performance. The list of stellar tenors stretches from Enrico Caruso and Francesco Tamagno early in the century to Beniamino Gigli, Giacomo Lauri Volpi, Jussi Bjoerling, Mario Del Monaco, Franco Corelli, Jan Peerce and Placido Domingo. By far the most frequent performers of Turiddu, however, were Frederick Jagel and Richard Tucker, both of whom sang it thirty-two times with the company. One very famous Canio, Giovanni Martinelli, never sang Turiddu at the Met, oddly enough, and neither did James McCracken.

So «Cavalleria rusticana» goes on its way with certain inevitability. The right work at the right time, it sparked the «verismo» movement - opera true to ordinary life - and introduced the short format, which quickly became an example for other composers, some of whose short operas - Richard Strauss' «Salome» and «Elektra», for example - seemed ad different from it as night from day. Popular appeal in its folklike melodies, a blunt story quickly told, earthen colors in the orchestra, hot sunshine in the singers' passionate outbursts - all these factors have made «Cavalleria rusticana» a permanent monument to its period and its audacious composer. His crusade to the New World may have brought him only a pack of troubles, but his most famous opera brought happiness to him and to listeners everywhere.

Pietro Mascagni, capricious youth in Leghorn, dissatisfied student at the Milan Conservatory, conductor of an operetta-company, maestro at Cerignola di Puglia.

Thriumphant victor at the Costanzi Theater in Rome, where he also will become a conductor, animator of three melodramatic tours through the United States and Argentina.

The composer Mascagni alternates, between successes, from his youthful experience «In filanda» to the experiment of «Nerone», going through verism with «Cavalleria rusticana» and the romanticism of «Guglielmo Ratcliff», from the fairy-tale «Iris» to the opera buffa «Le maschere», from «Parisina» to «Il Piccolo Marat».

CHRONOLOGY

1863 - Pietro Mascagni is born in Leghorn on the morning of December 7th.
1878 - First composition, the romance «Duolo», dedicated to his father.
1881 - First performance of the cantata «In filanda».
1882 - Final examination at the Milan Conservatory.
1885 - He starts his job as a conductor in operetta-companies.
1889 - Beginning of the composition of «Cavalleria rusticana».

1890 - «Cavalleria», after its victory during the Sonzogno-contest, triumphs at the Costanzi Theater in Rome.
1891 - Premiere of «L'Amico Fritz» in Rome.
1892 - Premiere of «I Rantzau» in Florence.
1895 - «Guglielmo Ratcliff» at La Scala in Milan. Mascagni is invited to direct the Liceo Musicale Rossini in Pesaro.
1896 - Premiere of the opera «Zanetto».

1898 - «Iris» at the Costanzi Theater in Rome.
1901 - «Le Maschere» on stage during the same evening in six different italian cities.
1905 - «Amica» in Montecarlo.
1909 - Mascagni becomes artistic director of the Costanzi Theater in Rome.
1911 - «Isabeau» in Genua and Buenos Aires.
1913 - «Parisina» at La Scala in Milano, libretto by D'Annunzio.

1915 - Musical soundtrack for the film «Rapsodia satanica».
1917 - «Lodoletta» in Rome.
1919 - The operetta «Sì» at the Quirino Theater in Rome.
1921 - First performance of «Il piccolo Marat» in Rome.
1929 - Mascagni is nominated «Accademico d'Italia».
1935 - «Nerone» at La Scala in Milano.
1945 - Mascagni dies on the morning of August 2nd.

THANKS

The authors are grateful to all those who have, with their precious collaboration, made it possible to achieve this monography. A special thanks to the Museo Teatrale alla Scala at Milan and its director Maestro Giampiero Tintori; the Mascagni Museum of Leghorn; the Scala Theater; the Comune of Leghorn; the Metropolitan of New York; the Houston Opera House; the editorial staff of the magazine «l'opera»; Roberto Del Nista; Umberto Bocca.

ICONOGRAPHICAL REFERENCES

(t/m/b = top/middle/below; l/c/r = left/center/right)

ARCHIVIO FOTOGRAFICO TEATRO ALLA SCALA: p. 13 b; p. 14 b; p. 18 b; p. 22 b; p. 23; p. 24.

ARCHIVIO RICORDI: p. 21 bl; p. 22 t; p. 37 t.

COLLEZIONE BERTARELLI: p. 6 t; p. 7 b; p. 17; p. 31 t; p. 33 t.

MUSEO MASCAGNI: p. 8; p. 9; p. 11 t-bl; p. 12 b; p. 14 t; p. 16; p. 19; p. 33 b; p. 35 t-br; p. 36 t; p. 37 b; p. 38; p. 39; p. 40 t.

MUSEO TEATRALE ALLA SCALA: p. 10 br; p. 15; p. 20; p. 27; p. 27 c; p. 29 tr; p. 31 b; p. 32; p. 34 t; p. 35 bl.

METROPOLITAN ARCHIVIO FOTOGRAFICO: p. 40 b; p. 41 t-d-r; p. 43.

RIVISTA «IL TEATRO ILLUSTRATO»: p. 6 t; p. 12 b; p. 13 c; p. 28.

RIVISTA «L'OPERA»: p. 18 t; p. 21 br; p. 25.

HOUSTON GRAND OPERA: p. 41, 42, 43, 44.

PHOTOGRAPHERS

Lelli & Masotti - Franco Fainello - Biserni - Umberto Bocca - De Rota - Foto «Arte» - Jese H. Hones Hall

Portraits of Greatness®

*SERIES I

**SERIES II

MOZART

VERDI

PUCCINI

ROSSINI

BEETHOVEN

PICTORIAL BIOGRAPHIES

This outstanding Series, illustrating the life and times of those great minds who forged our musical culture and heritage, is growing steadily. Each title in the Series faithfully recreates the atmosphere of the social, political and musical worlds of those times.

These books, richly illustrated in addition to being informative, have been welcomed by music lovers, educators, and students not only of music but of history.

Because their appeal is so universal we publish separate editions in English, French, Italian and German Editions in other languages are sometimes published by special arrangement.

Our books provide personal enrichment as well as popular supplementary education. They are the means whereby your experiences of live performances on stage or via your television screen can be confirmed in answering the questions that spring to mind about the composer — how he lived, where he lived, who helped him in time of need or obscurity — and why he lives on now, forever. ALL EDITIONS AVAILABLE SINGLY OR IN MULTIPLE CHOICE.

GIORDANO

CHOPIN

RESPIGHI

DANTE

GERSHWIN

MASCAGNI

TOSCANINI

*The First Series contains 50 titles copyrighted by Arnoldo Mondadori Editore in Milan, Italy, reprinted and translated by Elite Publishing Corp of New York

**Second Series created, designed and published by Treves Publishing Company in the style of the First Series

MAIL ORDER AND CHECK TO: ELITE PUBLISHING CORP.,11-03 46th Ave. — Long Island City, N.Y. 11101 5286

SERIES I-ELITE PUBLISHING,CORP.

PRICE PER COPY

SERIES II-TREVES PUBLISHING CO.

VERDI, English ☐, Italian ☐	$12.50
MOZART, English	$12.50
BEETHOVEN, English	$12.50
CHOPIN, English	$12.50
DANTE, English☐, Italian ☐	$12.50

PUCCINI, English, hardcover	$17.50
PUCCINI, English, softcover ☐	
Italian ☐, German ☐	$12.50
ROSSINI, English ☐, Italian ☐	$12.50
GIORDANO, English ☐, Italian ☐	$12.50
MASCAGNI, English ☐, Italian ☐	$12.50

RESPIGHI, English ☐, Italian ☐	$12.50
GERSHWIN, English, hardcover	$17.50
GERSHWIN, English, softcover	$12.50
TOSCANINI, English ☐, Italian ☐	$12.50
TOSCANINI, English ☐, hardcover	$17.50
MASCAGNI, English☐, hardcover	$17.50

POSTAGE AND HANDING FOR ONE COPY ORDER
$1.50 FOR EACH ADDITIONAL COPY $0.50 CHARGE

TOTAL ORDER: $

☐Charge my credit card
☐Master Card   ☐ Visa

Credit card no.   Expir. date

Name as it appears on card

NAME ....

ADDRESS ....

CITY ....

STATE ....ZIP CODF ....

TELEPHONE DAY ....EVENING ....

SIGNATURE

☐ CHECK ENCLOSED payable to: **ELITE PUBLISHING CORP.**

Portraits of Greatness®

*SERIES I   ****SERIES II**

MOZART

VERDI

PUCCINI

ROSSINI

BEETHOVEN

CHOPIN

DANTE

GIORDANO

RESPIGHI

GERSHWIN

PICTORIAL BIOGRAPHIES

This outstanding Series, illustrating the life and times of those great minds who forged our musical culture and heritage, is growing steadily. Each title in the Series faithfully recreates the atmosphere of the social, political and musical worlds of those times.

These books, richly illustrated in addition to being informative, have been welcomed by music lovers, educators, and students not only of music but of history.

Because their appeal is so universal we publish separate editions in English, French, Italian and German Editions in other languages are sometimes published by special arrangement.

Our books provide personal enrichment as well as popular supplementary education. They are the means whereby your experiences of live performances on stage or via your television screen can be confirmed in answering the questions that spring to mind about the composer — how he lived, where he lived, who helped him in time of need or obscurity — and why he lives on now, forever. ALL EDITIONS AVAILABLE SINGLY OR IN MULTIPLE CHOICE.

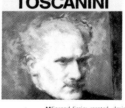
MASCAGNI

TOSCANINI

*The First Series contains 50 titles copyrighted by Arnoldo Mondadori Editore in Milan, Italy, reprinted and translated by Elite Publishing Corp of New York

**Second Series created, designed and published by Treves Publishing Company in the style of the First Series

---

MAIL ORDER AND CHECK TO: ELITE PUBLISHING CORP.,11-03 46th Ave. — Long Island City, N.Y. 11101 5286

SERIES I-ELITE PUBLISHING,CORP.

PRICE PER COPY

SERIES II-TREVES PUBLISHING CO.

VERDI, English ☐, Italian ☐ $12.50
MOZART, English $12.50
BEETHOVEN, English $12.50
CHOPIN, English $12.50
DANTE, English☐, Italian ☐ $12.50

PUCCINI, English, hardcover $17.50
PUCCINI,English, softcover ☐
Italian ☐, German ☐ $12.50
ROSSINI, English ☐, Italian ☐ $12.50
GIORDANO, English ☐, Italian ☐ $12.50
MASCAGNI, English ☐, Italian ☐ $12.50

RESPIGHI, English ☐, Italian ☐ $12.50
GERSHWIN, English, hardcover $17.50
GERSHWIN, English, softcover $12.50
TOSCANINI, English ☐, Italian ☐ $12.50
TOSCANINI, English ☐, hardcover $17.50
MASCAGNI, English☐, hardcover $17.50

POSTAGE AND HANDING FOR ONE COPY ORDER $1.50 FOR EACH ADDITIONAL COPY $0.50 CHARGE

TOTAL ORDER: $

☐Charge my credit card
☐Master Card   ☐ Visa

Credit card no.   Expir. date

Name as it appears on card

NAME ....

ADDRESS ....

CITY ....

STATE ....ZIP CODF ....

TELEPHONE DAY ....EVENING ....

SIGNATURE

☐ CHECK ENCLOSED payable to: **ELITE PUBLISHING CORP.**